GIRL, SNAP OUT OF IT!

GIRL, SNAP OUT OF IT!

⌒

STOP THE RELATIONSHIP MADNESS!

Kellie King

ISBN: 0692672222
ISBN 13: 9780692672228
Printed in the United States of America.

First Printing 2016

DISCLAIMER

INTRODUCTION

FIRST OFF, LET me share that I feel for you if you're in an unhealthy relationship or situation with someone. It's not fun. It can be so draining and take up so much mental space that you don't even notice life passing you by. It really sucks, and if you're reading this, it's likely you've given all or much of yourself and your attention to a man who treats you like crap in some way...or even in all ways.

Second, the most important thing to remember is that this book isn't about blaming your man—even if he's making your life miserable, even if he's rude, mean, aloof, distant, lazy, sneaky, a liar, a cheater, or all of the above. This is about getting your dignity and self-respect back, because anyone who stays with or pines over an undeserving man—putting him and his needs first—has a serious self-respect issue. This issue needs to be dealt with before you make any other decisions. Making decisions about your life and relationship from a place of weakness and insecurity is never a good thing, leading only to more bad decisions.

The great thing about your situation is that it's completely fixable! It could take a day, a month, or a year—that's up to you—but once you commit to figuring it out, you're on your way. Some women in your situation put up with bad relationships because they don't believe they can do better. Well, guess what? You can do better, and so can they. Being single is so much better than being with someone who doesn't cherish you—unless you don't cherish yourself, and in that case, being alone is just as bad or worse than enduring an unhealthy relationship.

If you don't love yourself, all your past, present, and future relationships reflect that. That's what this book is about—helping you get to a place where you're so happy with yourself and have so much self-respect that nothing and nobody will ever be able to take that away from you again.

The reason I'm writing this book is because I've been there. I've been through a frustrating, demeaning relationship, and I've watched so many of the smartest, most beautiful, most talented women I've ever met go through the same thing. They went from being confident, powerful, happy people to lost, pitiful, miserable shells of their former selves—all over an exasperating relationship that completely depleted their self-worth.

I wasted a lot of time acting pathetic—crying, blaming, getting back together, breaking up, and driving my close friends crazy to the point where they didn't want to hear one more word about my relationship. The few who did keep listening were going through the same unhealthy patterns as I was, so we fed off one another's misery. It felt better to vent and feel sorry for ourselves than it did to sit alone with our obsessive thoughts about the last stupid text war or bad conversation.

The most frustrating part for me was that, up until that point, I had never gotten overly invested in relationships. I didn't care about having a boyfriend. I broke up with someone if I didn't like the way he dressed or if he said something stupid. I never got what all the whining love songs were about, and I used to make fun of my friends for crying over breakups. Maybe I was a late bloomer, because when I fell in love for the first time at twenty-six years old, I was singing Barry Manilow songs and crying after every stupid fight. Overnight I had become one of those girls I'd made fun of in the past—and I actually loved it. It was fun to be in love...until the craziness began.

This book is not about getting him back or making him love you and treat you right. (Although when you change, it will change the way your partner sees you, and in many cases, the relationship will completely turn around.) The focus of this book is to look at the reason you're letting yourself become a nutjob over a man. Why do you think you need a man who isn't 100 percent into you? Why are you waiting around and hoping he'll change when he clearly has no intention of committing to you or being good to you? Or why do you stick with him when he plays games and is available one day but not the next? FYI, halfway committed or partially committed is *not committed.*

I'm not going to sugarcoat anything, so some things I say might seem harsh. But my only goal here is to get you to *snap out of it!* After watching so many women go through completely dysfunctional, degrading relationships with men, many of whom weren't even worth losing a moment's sleep over, I decided I would never let that happen to me again.

One night after getting off the phone with a crying friend, who was going through yet another breakup with the same guy for the hundredth time, it became crucial for me to learn why so many women in relationships end up like this. I began what would become an intensive study into codependency and insecurity in relationships. It was all very fascinating to me, but a lot of the information I was finding completely blamed the man. The "experts" writing many of these books and articles described narcissistic/codependent relationships and said it was impossible to form a meaningful union with a man who exhibits narcissistic traits. That just didn't make sense to me. Find me a man (or woman) with zero narcissistic traits and I'll show you my pet unicorn. Yes, there are different degrees of narcissism, but I refused to believe that putting selfish or inconsiderate men in a category and writing them off was the answer. There are two people in a relationship, and even if the guy is a jerk, doesn't the woman join in this madness? Doesn't the way she communicates her feelings or the fact that she continues to stay with a man who isn't treating her well (while hoping he'll change) play a part in the dysfunction?

It would have been easy to blame these men, and for a while I did because I just wanted to feel better. But the more I read, the less it made sense. I knew something needed to change in the way we girls react. Nobody is supposed to have that much control over someone else's emotions, but it was happening to so many women I knew. We typically tried to figure out our "stupid" guys but spent no time looking at why we were acting like a bunch of needy little drama queens, never even realizing our codependent, pathetic ways of communicating were part of the problem.

We weren't physically tied up and unable to get away. We willingly let this happen to us while constantly bitching about it. We did this to ourselves—letting men disrespect us over and over and then whining about it and looking to them to fix it.

I went to a shrink during the height of my confusion in my relationship, thinking maybe she could figure this out for me. She told me I was addicted to an unavailable man and that it was my dad's fault or something predictably unoriginal like that. I wanted to believe her because, again, I just wanted to feel better.

I'm sure there *was* a link in my childhood as to why I acted like such a mess over a guy who didn't seem all that serious about me, but something was missing. I mean, it doesn't take a genius to know that acting pathetic and desperate is unattractive. Even if he was being an ass, wasn't it partly my fault for putting up with it? He wasn't unavailable—he was just not very interested in *me* anymore. Well, he was interested sometimes, and other times just enough to have some fun when he felt like it.

So after two uninspiring shrink sessions, I left, determined to figure out how to get my confidence back on my own. I dived into reading books about communicating in relationships and learning what a healthy relationship is. I read every book I could find, watched videos, and read countless articles about behavior, codependency, communication, and so on.

I slowly began looking at my relationship differently. I stopped obsessing and put myself first. What he did and how he acted wasn't really my concern anymore. I also gave my friends advice about what I was learning instead of getting sucked into drama-filled conversations about the latest disrespectful thing someone's man had done. Somehow I became the person to call when women I knew were having relationship troubles.

Friends gave my number to *their* friends who were having problems with men. It was always the same complaints: "He doesn't want to commit." "He's so mean to me." "He loves me, but he's not available." "He's hot and then cold." "He starts a fight or disappears whenever I bring up the future."

It's been several years since I had that light bulb moment. I'm now happily married to a man who "wouldn't commit." My friends threw me a wedding shower, and because they thought it would never happen, the invitation they made had a flying pig on it!

They all thought he and I would get married "when pigs fly," as the saying goes. That's how far he and I have come. And if I hadn't figured out what was going on with *me*—fixing my (pathetic, needy) codependency issues, learning to communicate, and gaining respect for myself—I would still be going through the same BS...whether with him or in *any* future relationships. Believe me,

I'm still far from perfect, but I'll never go back to that pathetic place where I feel desperate or needy in my relationship.

What I'm going to try to drill into your head in this book is so incredibly simple it can be hard to grasp at first. I'm going to explain it in as many ways as I can think of. I give examples of some of the amazing, beautiful, smart, funny, successful yet incredibly frustratingly pathetic-acting (myself included) ladies, young and not so young, I've known over the past several years. Some got dumped, some did the dumping, and some married the "pain in the ass." But the ones who were determined to grow and learn and take back control of their lives are now so much stronger after relearning how to love themselves and stop being doormats. Feeling weak and insecure is *so* draining. Being strong, confident, and fun is the goal here. It's actually really easy because you were born that way. You just forgot!

There's one little disclaimer I will continue to mention: this is not a book on how to get your ex-boyfriend, ex-husband, ex-booty call, or ex-anything back. A lot of you are with really selfish guys who don't deserve you. If he's predominantly lazy, rude, perverted, mean, snappy, condescending, or abusive, he's probably not worth any more of your time. Every single woman who's in an unhealthy relationship gave her power over to a man at some point. Those who realize that and take back their power move on or become stronger and more confident...with or without a man.

Life is meant to be enjoyed with people who want to be with you and you feel good around. That said, when you really love and take care of yourself, people around you see that and rise to meet you...or slither away to find people who will meet them down on their level.

"Here's all you have to know about men and women: women are crazy, men are stupid. And the main reason women are crazy is that men are stupid."

— (GEORGE CARLIN)

The above quote is obviously not 100 percent accurate, but it's funny.

CHAPTER 1

MY JOURNEY THROUGH PATHETICVILLE

I'LL START THIS book with my own gut-wrenchingly embarrassing relationship disaster stories. When I look back at how dramatic it all was, it seems I'm writing about someone else. I was such a mess, and I wasted so much time on years of nonsense!

It didn't seem like nonsense at the time, though. It was all very tragic and melodramatic.

If you've ever thought you'll never find another man as wonderful as the man you're crying over, let me just say, "Hell, yes, you will!" I thought I might literally die from dehydration because tears would not stop falling from my eyeballs after "Matt" told me he couldn't be with me anymore.

I met Matt at a barbecue a mutual friend was hosting. I had just gotten out of a very long, very wrong relationship and wanted to meet someone new. I had never been in love and really wanted to know what it was like. Matt was quiet, sweet, and responsible, and he had a big group of fun friends and an awesome job. He was the exact opposite of my loud, rude, bad-boy ex, and that seemed perfect. We talked all night and both knew we would see more of each other. I wouldn't give him my number, but I took his and waited a few days to call him. He picked up on the first ring and said, "Kellie?" He knew who it was because of my area code and said he had been waiting for me to call. He had no game, and I liked that a lot.

From then on, we were inseparable. He brought me breakfast on his way to work every morning when he didn't stay over. He organized my bills and paperwork, washed my car, and invited me to do everything he did. I wasn't "in love" yet, but he was so sweet and attentive. I really loved being with him.

Before I met Matt, I had been thinking of moving to Hawaii. I'd lived on Oahu when I was younger and had recently been offered a great job opportunity there. I had a trip planned to stay with a friend for two weeks to check it out and see if moving back was the best option. Matt was really upset when I left. He thought I'd never come back and that he'd lost me. While I was away, I really missed him. I realized I was in love and couldn't leave him. When I got home, Matt was beyond happy, and I was excited to be in love! I told him about my revelation, and we immediately got serious.

Not long after this newfound bliss, things took a peculiar turn. At least, my actions became peculiar. One morning after Matt left for work, I woke up and decided to clean his entire house, do his laundry, and make dinner. I hadn't been to my house in days, was between jobs, and was completely neglecting my own life and focusing on his. When he came home for lunch and saw I was still there scrubbing the bathroom, I could tell he was wondering what the hell had come over me. I was not a cleaner. I hated cleaning, and although he was thankful, he was kind of unpleasantly surprised by my newfound desire to make his life better and avoid my own. That didn't stop me, though!

Things just got worse from there. I was in love, so that meant I was supposed to constantly show him how I felt, right? I decided he was the most amazing man in the world, and I took every chance I could to show him and tell him. FYI, he was kind of a nerd and not exactly a catch by any normal standards. More than a few people asked what I saw in him. I didn't care. I was "in love" and had decided Matt was the only man for me. I didn't care that he was cheap or that he had yellow teeth. I overlooked the fact that he drank way too much on the weekends and went MIA sometimes.

I'd decided he was perfect and that we were meant to be. I spent less and less time with my friends. I came home from my new job and waited to hear from him before I made any plans. His laundry was always ready for him, and I made sure I always looked perfect. I was pretty much as pathetic as a girl can get.

It never even occurred to me that he wasn't overjoyed with my neediness and codependency. Never for a moment was I aware that I'd become so pathetic and annoying that he would want to break up with me. I wanted to see what being in love was like, and I did. I was so good at it! My life revolved around him. Wasn't that love? Who wouldn't appreciate that? So when he came to my house after having dinner with friends one night and said he couldn't be with me anymore, I didn't believe him. Only when he took his things from my closet did it really start to hit me.

Well, that's when everything got really ridiculous. I was in shock. It was like a death, and I literally couldn't function. He called to tell me he was coming to get the rest of his things. *What? But we're so in love! This cannot be true.* I could barely respond.

I hadn't cried yet because I kept thinking there was some mistake, that he couldn't possibly want to be without me. I put his clothes in a plastic bag and had a brilliant idea. I would spray my perfume all over them, and that would make him think of me and miss me so much he'd realize his mistake. I left the clothes outside and got a text from him a little while later. It read, "Did you spray perfume all over my clothes? That's really weird. I had to put everything in the wash." So my genius plan had actually irritated him. That was when I knew he was definitely gone.

I cried for weeks. I didn't let him know how devastated I was, but I couldn't eat or sleep. My friends couldn't believe I was such a mess over a guy who wasn't even my type and who I normally wouldn't have given so much as a second glance. I tried to get my mind off him, but nothing worked. I was a wreck. Then to make matters worse, he started calling. He told me he missed me but then went snowboarding with a bunch of people and didn't invite me. He came by and said he wished we were together but then disappeared for a week. I still didn't go out with friends. I just stayed home and waited for him to call. We ended up dating again, but things never got better. He was detached, and I was miserably trying to make it work. I was so preoccupied with this stupid relationship that one night, while riding my bike home, I didn't notice a red light at an intersection. I rode right into traffic and was hit by a car! I spent the night in the hospital and, luckily, only had a few cuts and bruises.

While I tortured myself, Matt was having the time of his life. He was more than happy to have me sitting at home. I was miserable, waiting for attention from him, while he was out having a great time. Finally, I decided I couldn't take it anymore. I was going back to my plan of moving to Hawaii. It had been less than a year since I'd met Matt, and it had gone from being one of the best years of my life to the worst.

The move to Hawaii was the right thing to do. I'm not suggesting anyone run away from their problems, but my job offer was still available, and I was grateful to have something else to focus on. While in Hawaii, I was still very hung up on Matt. He called and told me he loved me and he wanted to come get me and take me back. He was obviously full of crap. He just wanted to make sure I didn't forget about him. I wound up not taking the job but instead started a little health-food restaurant and just kept busy. I made some great friends, got myself together, and about a year later, met Paul.

I wasn't totally over the Matt drama when I met Paul, but the second I saw him, I knew I was in trouble. He was pretty much everything I love in a man—handsome, funny, very generous, driven, and full of life. I was still dealing with residual "patheticness" from my relationship with Matt, but I knew right away I wanted to get to know Paul. I hadn't even noticed another man in over a year, so I definitely wasn't looking. But from the moment we met, there were serious fireworks. I hadn't dealt with my codependency issues at all, and I still had no idea why Matt and I hadn't worked out. So getting into another relationship was pretty scary. I didn't think I had done anything wrong in the unraveling of my relationship with Matt. In fact, I thought I was the perfect girlfriend. So why get involved with someone I really liked if he could just dump me for no reason?

It was unavoidable, however. Paul was so much fun. He lived in California and spent a lot of time in Hawaii. When he was away, we talked on the phone so much that he sent me a headset so I could make food and talk without putting my neck against my shoulder to hold the phone. (That was before unlimited phone plans, so we had to use landlines.) He wrote me a hilarious song and recorded it in his music studio. He sent me '80s mix CDs for my restaurant, and whenever I went to California or he came to Hawaii, we were together. I eventually sold my business and got a great job offer in California. I loved Hawaii but missed being close to my friends and family.

Going home was the beginning of some serious turmoil with Paul. We fought a lot. He wasn't really committed, and I felt we weren't going anywhere. When not fighting, we had so much fun together. We'd be together every day for a week, and then he would say, "I'm going to Hawaii for three weeks." There was no invite, no discussion, just, "See ya." At this point, I was such a mess from my last relationship that instead of talking or communicating I just pretended I didn't care and felt sorry for myself. Or some days I would have a meltdown, yelling and calling him names. He had tons of female friends, most of whom were not nice to me. I was weirded out and uncomfortable, but I stayed silent for the most part. If it got really bad, I blew up. There was no in between and no discussion about anything. I had only two reactions: freak out or avoid.

We fought by e-mail for days. He knew I shared the e-mails with my friends, so he always wrote, "Hi, Shelly!" to my best friend at the end of an e-mail war. It was actually pretty funny but also incredibly frustrating. Paul had gone through a bad divorce a few years before he met me, and he was obviously apprehensive about committing again. We loved each other so much, but we couldn't get on the same page. We must have broken up fifty times. He was a master at avoiding commitment, and I was a master at feeling sorry for myself. This went on for years. Even when we weren't talking, we texted each other funny pictures and commented when we saw something that reminded us of each other. We always got back together, but nothing really changed.

Finally, one day I'd had enough. Nothing was working. My bitching, crying, avoiding, whining, angry texting approach was not—and never had been—a success. I saw myself doing the same thing in twenty years, never getting anywhere or just getting dumped again. I decided what he was doing and who he was doing it with was not my problem anymore. I was free. It wasn't anything I said or did—I just stopped blaming him. I loved him, and I wanted the best for him, even if that meant not being together. No more feeling sorry for myself or needing him to change to make me happy. He knew what I wanted, and if he wasn't interested in fully committing, it was time to move on.

That's when everything changed. We actually broke up for several months, and for the first time in a long time, I was happy. I missed him, but I knew what I wanted and would not get sucked back into an unhealthy relationship. That was the longest we had ever been apart, and we completely stopped communicating. I moved on and assumed Paul had too. Months later when we finally did get in touch, things were much different. I was serious about what I wanted, and Paul had done a lot of thinking. He came back and showed me he was ready to commit. He did a 180, completely stepping up. A year later we were married.

As mentioned, before I changed my thinking and snapped out of it, I had, over the years, had some unsuccessful shrink encounters, read tons of books on relationships, and devoured any material I could find, trying to understand my part in the dysfunction. I had been acting like a victim, feeling sorry for myself and blaming others when I was the only one who really needed to change. I learned how to communicate without whining and the difference between asking for what I wanted as opposed to bitching. I also realized that letting go of someone doesn't have to be dramatic and devastating. If you don't look at letting go of someone as the end, but a new beginning, life becomes exciting again. You might have moments of sadness, but they won't last because you've chosen to believe that something better is coming.

It's so easy to blame someone else when things go wrong, especially if something he does drives you crazy. But the bottom line is you have a choice. When you decide to stop feeling sorry for yourself and blaming someone else, you make room to grow and learn from your behavior. Everything is *not* everyone else's fault. If someone is treating you poorly and all you do is bitch and whine or, even worse, pretend you're fine and then blow up when you can't take it anymore, you remain in victim mode. You have a choice, and now is the time to choose. Are you ready to *snap out of it* and take your life back?

⌒

"Nobody can hurt me without my permission."

— (GANDHI)

⌒

CHAPTER 2

YOU MIGHT BE ACTING PATHETIC IF...

MAYBE YOU AREN'T really sure if you qualify as "pathetic" in your relationships with men. I've come up with the following real-life examples of possible scenarios you might be familiar with that should help clarify your position. Unfortunately, even some very smart women act like hot messes when it comes to relationships.

You might be acting pathetic if…

- Your mood is determined by how your man acts toward you.
- You habitually break up with him. You tell him and your friends you're done, that you're too good for his BS. Three hours, or days, later, he calls and you act like nothing happened.
- You're with a guy who gets weird when you bring up any discussion about the future. You try to act cool but blow up after he avoids any commitment conversation for the millionth time. This makes him disappear because he avoids confrontation. You quickly go back to the noncommittal arrangement while quietly feeling used.
- You spend ridiculous amounts of time stalking his and his friends' social media.

- You put plans with friends on hold because you're waiting to see if he wants to do something with you first.
- You dump him because he doesn't treat you right, but you continue letting him booty call you, which makes his treatment of you actually worse than before because now he gets to sleep with you with zero commitment.
- You continue having sex with a guy who clearly isn't even that into you because it's the only time he's affectionate toward you.
- You're with a guy who has a wife or girlfriend.
- You stay with a guy who says he doesn't want to get married or have kids even though you want to get married and have kids.
- The guy you're dating doesn't invite you to do things with his friends or family, rarely takes you to dinner, and never surprises you with gifts (aside from a possible STD).
- You're madly in love with a guy who has no money, lives with his parents, and lets you pay for all or most meals and occasionally his cell phone bill. (If the cell payment hasn't happened yet, it will.)
- The weird guy you're kind of dating just because you don't want to be alone sends you pictures of his "junk." You're grossed out but don't say anything and you keep dating him.

These are just a few scenarios you might be able to relate to if you're acting pathetic. I borrowed all of the above examples from actual girls I know. If you can identify with any of these situations, don't feel bad. You just got a little lost and made a man more important than yourself. It's easy to fix.

"If you live for people's acceptance, you'll die from their rejection."

— (Lecrae)

Another less obvious way you could be acting pathetic is what I call SYM syndrome—(unintentionally) smother your man syndrome.

Are you scaring him off? Could your actions be the reason why he blows you off or doesn't want to commit?

If you're acting desperate or emotionally needy, you're likely freaking him out. The problem is a lot of women don't realize that they're acting desperate. You could be doing little subtle things that push him away or make him think you're needy or high maintenance. SYM syndrome can happen out of the blue. Everything could be going great and then boom, he starts to withdraw and you have no clue why. A woman might think she's being loving, caring, and affectionate when she's really being annoying and smothering. Men will rarely voice their feelings when they're irritated with a woman who gives up too much of herself or becomes clingy. He'll just withdraw, become distant, and suddenly be too "busy" for a relationship. Things might start out great, but after a few weeks or months of you gushing over him, you might start to hear things like, "I really like/love you, but I'm just not ready for a relationship" or "I've got too much going on right now" or "You're amazing, but…" Maybe you're in a committed relationship but you want to get married. If you've become a little too clingy or overly dependent on him and he starts pulling away, don't expect a ring until you snap out of it!

Here are some multiple-choice questions that will help you pinpoint ways you might be acting desperate and sabotaging a perfectly good or potential relationship with SYM syndrome...

1. Your boyfriend tells you he's tired and doesn't want to come over to your house tonight. He's had a long day and just wants to go to bed early.

    A. You get upset and ask him why he can't just sleep at your house. You get emotional and whine until he says he'll come over. Then you tell him you don't want him to come over now because you only want him to come if he wants to.
    B. You say, "No problem," and act like you're fine, but you're really upset because you can't understand why he would rather sleep alone than with you. You secretly hold onto this issue until he does something that, in your eyes, proves he loves you again.
    C. You say, "No problem," tell him to get a good night's sleep, and make a funny joke like, "That's too bad, though. I booked a hot Swedish massage therapist for us tonight. Don't worry. Get some sleep. I'll send pics." He goes to bed laughing. You then make plans or stay home and have a great night because your contentment has nothing to do with your boyfriend. Plus, you enjoy your alone time, so it worked out great.

Can you tell which one of these would make a guy feel like he's with an awesome, secure woman? Can you tell what would be annoying and smothering for a guy who just wants to get some sleep and spend some time alone? Women tend to read into everything. A man saying he wants to stay home rather than come over to your house might be translated to "I don't want to be near you ever again and I don't love you anymore" by a woman with a severe case of SYM syndrome. Turn your SYM into LIG (let it go) and give yourself and him the freedom to enjoy each other.

⌒

"If [he] was meant to be controlled, [he] would have come with a remote."

— (GENEREUX PHILIP)

⌒

2. The guy you're seeing asks you to check on his house and feed his fish while he's on a work trip. You like him a lot, but he hasn't committed to you completely or called you his girlfriend. His house is not close to your house or your work, so it's kind of a pain in the butt.

A. You tell him he can bring his fish over to your house, but you might not be able to make it over to his house while he's gone. You lightheartedly tell him your housesitting fees are pretty hefty too, so it would make more sense to bring the fish to you and lock up his house really well.

B. You get excited because you think this is a sign that he wants to get more serious. You say yes and not only feed his fish, but clean and organize his entire house and buy him new sheets and towels too.

C. You don't want to say no because you want to show him how helpful you are. It's a hassle for you, but you tell him you'll just stay at his house while he's gone.

I don't think it's ever a good idea to do big favors for someone you're dating when he has yet to show you he's committed.

Answer A seems OK because you're making him put some effort into what he's asking. You aren't going out of your way, but if he wants to bring his fish over, you'll be glad to help.

Answers B and C are for someone who needs SYM boot camp. He might not be committing because he's already sensed you're a pushover. He should feel lucky to be with you, but if you're going out of your way and trying to please him before he's even gotten serious, you're showing him you value him and what might make him happy before yourself and your needs. That's not attractive. You don't have to be a bitch, but you do have to know your self-worth and never ever chase a man or do things you're not comfortable with just to please him.

$\backsim$

"Stop chasing what your mind wants and you'll get what your soul needs."

— (UNKNOWN)

$\backsim$

3. You really like the man you're dating. He starts to hint that he wants you to be his girlfriend. Although he doesn't exactly act like your dream guy yet, you...

A. Post pictures of yourself and him on social media and say things like "my man" and "this guy" and change your relationship status ASAP. Meanwhile, he hasn't even acknowledged you on social media aside from maybe a tag.

B. Stop hanging out with your friends and wait around for him to call or text. You don't miss your friends because he's pretty much the only thing you really think about.

C. Don't care. Since he hasn't officially asked you to be his girlfriend, you're single and you keep your options open. You make plans with your friends before you talk to him and don't "claim him" in any way. If he isn't your dream guy, who cares?

I see answer A all the time. I just saw a post the other day from a girl I know that read, "He's leaving me for a work trip on my birthday!" with a picture of her boyfriend and sad-face emojis. Why would anyone post that? Does she think people need to know her relationship issues? Needless to say she doesn't feel appreciated, but she sure keeps chasing him anyway. Meanwhile, he rarely posts photos of them together or acknowledges her on his wall. Maybe he feels like he doesn't have to put much effort in because she's obsessed enough for both of them. My advice to her would be to reel it back and relax. If you don't like the lack of effort, calmly tell him, and if he doesn't want to change, move on. Don't complain to the world about it and feel sorry for yourself.

Answer B usually goes along with answer A, but not everyone posts their lives on social media. The point of both is to show that when your life revolves around someone else, you're acting pathetic. Don't put effort into someone who doesn't put effort into you.

Answer C is a healthy answer that a confident girl would give. Even if you adore this guy, if it happens, it happens. Don't force it or stress about it, and don't chase him! Don't chase a man you're dating, don't chase your boyfriend, and, even if you're married, don't chase your husband. It just isn't cute.

He used to be so sweet!

CHAPTER 3

HE USED TO BE SO SWEET

"BUT HE USED to love me so much!"

I'm guessing your relationship wasn't always such a mess. When you first met, there was tons of chemistry. He pursued you, was always interested in you, called and texted all the time, and told you how amazing you are. Maybe he even got to the point where he told you he loved you. Then a few months down the road, the fairy tale turned into a bad drama. Most of the time, you can think back and remember a weird fight, an event, or something that changed the course of your relationship—a "red flag" moment.

The following story is about Kathy and Jason. Your relationship might not be as dramatic as theirs, or maybe it's more dramatic, but these are two people who don't know how to communicate. Kathy becomes an emotional wreck trying to make Jason treat her right.

When they met, it was instant attraction. Kathy hadn't dated anyone for a long time because she was focused on her career. She didn't really care about dating, and she seemed really confident and fine with being single, but meeting Jason changed all that. He was handsome and driven, and he was all up in Kathy's business from day one. Flowers, dates every night, and, after a month, he flew to Texas to meet Kathy's parents. She was so happy. She thought she'd found "the one" and couldn't stop talking about how awesome Jason was. Everyone was really happy for her. But not long after getting back from Texas, things changed.

For Kathy, the first of many red flags happened when she and Jason went on a snowboarding trip with some of his friends. She was a beginner, but everyone else was experienced. She assumed that when they got to the mountain, Jason would help her and teach her how to snowboard like he'd promised. When they got off the ski lift for the first time, however, Jason took off with everyone else and left Kathy to fumble down the mountain on her own. When she finally got to the bottom of the hill, Jason was talking to a cute girl in the lift line. Kathy was bummed, but she kept it together and got in line with them.

When she scooted up to Jason, he barely acknowledged her and kept talking to the other girl. Kathy was shocked. She'd thought this vacation was going to be the best trip ever. In less than a day, it had turned into a nightmare. Kathy didn't want to make a scene, so she decided to hold back her feelings until later when they went back to the cabin.

When they got on the ski lift, Kathy asked Jason for some pointers to help her down the hill. He looked at her and said, "I didn't come here just to sit on the mountain and babysit. Why don't you just go take a lesson?" Well, that did it. Kathy went ballistic, crying and yelling, and fought with him the remainder of the vacation. Prior to that trip, she'd had no idea Jason even had a selfish or rude bone in his body. Most girls would have told Jason to shove his board up his ass and left, but Kathy was pretty whipped. She thought maybe Jason was having a bad day or was stressed out.

Jason turned out to be totally manipulative, and with every fight they had, Kathy's IQ seemed to drop a little. She got into a pattern of breaking up with him and saying they were done, but three hours later she was usually on her way to his house with a frickin' basket of cookies and wearing a new lace bra and panty set. The next day it would be like nothing had happened.

She called me at 3:00 a.m. just to read me her latest genius text response, which was finally gonna make him see his wrongs and the need to change. He stormed out for the dumbest reasons, like if she put too much salt in the dinner she'd made him. Kathy also had a flair for drama. She once threw dirt in his face in front of their friends, and another time she wore a wig and staked out his apartment for hours because she was sure he was cheating. She told him she missed her period just to see what he would say if she were pregnant.

"If you keep telling the same sad small story, you will keep living the same sad small life."

— (JEAN HOUSTON)

Kathy stayed in that mess of a relationship for two years. Jason constantly put her down and flirted with other girls. He always found stupid reasons to get into fights, and she often found out he just wanted to go somewhere without having to invite her and was starting fights as his "escape route." He even told her he would like her more if she were to surf and do more sports. Kathy held on to her vision of what she wanted Jason to be. She was still in love with the guy Jason had acted like when they'd first met, so she spent two years hoping she could change him back to Mr. Wonderful.

Finally, Jason completely stopped communicating with Kathy. She tried to keep the drama going, but he was done manipulating her. Even though he'd instigated much of the drama, it became too much and he was done. Kathy was devastated. They had a routine. He did something mean or stupid, she broke up with him, they'd miss each other, and they'd get back together—that was the drill. She was supposed to be the one to break up, and eventually he would change his evil ways and see the light. It took months for her to come to terms with the final breakup.

Kathy looks back at that time and cannot believe how crazy she got over Jason. She lost entire days over text wars. She stayed up all night crying if he didn't call. Her work suffered, and after he cut her off, she had to move across town just to get away from all the memories of those last two years with him.

If Kathy hadn't held on to the fantasy of the guy Jason had pretended to be when they met, she would have told him to get lost when he ditched her and flirted with the girl on that ski trip. She can't believe how much time she wasted on him. She let herself fall under a really dysfunctional spell, and now that she's free, she's very careful not to let it happen again.

⌒

**"Breakups aren't always meant for makeups.
Sometimes they're meant for wakeups."**

— (UNKNOWN)

⌒

CHAPTER 4

GETTING TIRED OF THE DRAMA

"I'M EXHAUSTED FROM trying to make him want me, love me, approve of me..."

If you've gotten to this point, you're full-on driving yourself insane over your relationship. Maybe you're trying to be cool and let him do his own thing, but you feel miserable in your silence. Or maybe you blow up every time he disses you or treats you as if you aren't important to him.

This is basically the crossroads in a relationship. You're both stuck because he's content the way things are, while you're trying to get to the next level. This can go on for years. You fight, e-mail, text, and repeat the same things over and over in a million different ways to try to get your point across to him. Usually you stop talking or break up, but after a few weeks or months, you miss each other and get back together, thinking things are going to be different. Then a week back into the relationship, you realize he hasn't changed a bit. So you repeat the same pattern. You play it cool, going along like everything's great. You go out of your way for him. You even do things that aren't that fun or are a waste of your time just to hang out with him. Soon, he does something rude and disrespectful or says something that causes you to question his real feelings, and you once again realize you're definitely not a priority to him. So...you go back to breaking up or ignoring each other. Then he's nice or sends a funny text or you need to tell him something, and next thing you know, you're back to your insignificant role as doormat or on the booty-call roller coaster.

You get to a point where you're arguing with him in your head all the time, trying to get your point across, to make him finally understand so he'll want to commit or treat you better. You argue and talk to yourself while driving to work or before you go to sleep. You've turned into a complete nutjob, and you know things have to change. Well, *hopefully* you know that. None of your long, drawn-out, emotional, heart-wrenching conversations get through to him because he doesn't want to hear it.

If you're playing it cool, acting so laid-back like it doesn't bother you when he ignores you or seems too busy to spend time with you, you're not fooling anyone. Men smell desperation just like women can tell when a man is desperate.

You can act as cool as you want—it won't matter. He's on to you.

So how do you stop this insanity?

So many women go through this, and *many* get stronger from it and vow to never again act like that over a man. You'll rise above it, and when you do, you'll laugh at what an ass you were—over a guy! And that's OK. It's funny to look back. I love hearing and telling stories of the ridiculous things girls have said and done to try to keep or please a man. Some are so gross I wouldn't even write them in this book. I mean, it can take really embarrassing and sometimes nasty stuff just to keep him interested, but it's hilarious to get together with a group of girls and tell the stories. Kristen Wiig in the movie *Bridesmaids* is pretty hilarious with a guy she's seeing, and it's a great example of how dumb girls can act to keep a guy. If you're one of the two women on the planet who hasn't seen the film, please rent it or download it.

Everyone's limit for that kind of insanity varies. For most, the drama feeds the insane cycle. Once you realize it's all just drama, it becomes clear these intense, repetitive conversations are going nowhere. If you're the "play it cool" type, you might realize you're only his booty call and prolonging your misery. Even if he tells you he loves you or wants to commit, what are his actions saying? You'll see through his words the moment you decide to take responsibility for the situation you've put yourself in.

It's really *not* the man's fault. He's just a horny guy with an ego. If you're willing to stay and give him what he wants, he's a happy camper! Don't blame him when you choose to make yourself available to him. You've put your little ass on a nice, shiny platter and served him up a big slice of pathetic pie. If you're going to stay and wait around for him like a little puppy, hoping he'll magically turn into the man of your dreams, he'll likely put up with your little tantrums until one of you finally pulls the plug. No man wants a desperate, sad, pathetic, easy woman. He'll stay and tell you bits and pieces of what you want to hear, treating you exactly how you let him, until he gets bored and finds a more interesting challenge.

A really good guy friend of mine once told me that when a man really wants to be with a woman, nothing in the world can stop him. That turns out to be true. You can always tell when a man really cares about you. If he's just too busy…or puts you down… or treats you like an afterthought…or attends important events without inviting you…or changes plans last minute…or says he's too tired to see you…or does any of the above on a consistent basis, he does *not* respect you. He only wants to be with you when it's convenient for him, and he'll treat you well only when he wants something. That's not a relationship, and *you can do better.*

As one of my funniest friends, who finally "snapped out of it," says, "He was consistently partially there for me." She actually said those words, and when she heard herself say them, she woke up from her self-induced man spell and dumped the guy.

If you've gotten this far in this book, congratulations—you're ready to break your man spell. Don't try to do it cold turkey unless you really know you're done. In my experience with women who say they're going to cut it off abruptly, they usually throw a few degrading booty calls in before they really wake up and leave for good. If that happens to you, don't beat yourself up. Just get back to your goal of treating yourself with respect and paying attention to his actions, not his words.

"Never love anybody who treats you like you're ordinary."

— (OSCAR WILDE)

Be the observer, not the pursuer. Is he saying one thing and doing another? Do you constantly whine to him, text him, or feel sorry for yourself because he doesn't treat you the way you want him to? That's a waste of time and exhausting for both of you, so catch yourself when you nag. It's pointless because nagging is not communicating. It only makes you feel worse. Go easy on yourself... and him. It took you a while to get this sucked in. This is a habit for you, and part of you really thinks to be happy you need this guy in your life. I hear things like, "He's really a sweet guy" or "He's just not ready yet" or "I know he loves me" or "I'm not gonna find anyone better than him." Um...stop it! If he's so great and loves you so much, why are you so miserable?

Stand up for *yourself*! Put *yourself* first! Take care of *yourself*! When you stop needing him and quit acting like a desperate, pathetic little doormat, you'll clearly see what kind of disrespectful behavior this guy really is exhibiting. Maybe he's just a jerk and he'll try to get you back in his web a few more times. If he really is a jerk, he'll never change, and when he sees you're serious about respecting yourself, he'll find another sucker. Maybe he's a good guy and you were just freaking him out with your desperate neediness and whining. He might see you differently and treat you right when you stop obsessing over him and practice putting yourself first. If that happens, *you* decide if you really want him.

Sorry if it seems I'm being harsh, but I really want you to absorb what I'm saying. Nobody wants to be with someone who doesn't respect herself. It's a major turnoff. If you're with a guy—good or bad—he'll treat you only as good as you treat yourself. People who love themselves don't put up with games and disrespect. They don't bother with nonsense.

Please, stop being pathetic. Focus on you, get a life, and snap out of it!

⌒

"The first step toward getting somewhere is to decide that you are not going to stay where you are."

— (J. P. Morgan)

⌒

He's consistently partially there for me

CHAPTER 5

HE'S CONSISTENTLY PARTIALLY THERE FOR ME

"HE'S CONSISTENTLY PARTIALLY there for me."

That's my favorite "pathetic" quote from my friend Stella, who spent years making excuses for her one-sided relationship. I mention that quote a few times in this book because it so beautifully sums up the relationship of a girl who needs to snap out of it. Women think that if a man has said or done some nice things for them, he must really care. I've listened to girls bring up something a man did for them years earlier as proof he's a good guy; those girls just aren't ready to let go yet.

Stella dated the same man on and off for five years. She had all these wonderful things to say about him, but she was clearly not happy with the relationship. She said she could rely on him, that he was a really good person, and that he was her "rock." I asked, "If he's so great, why are you upset?"

She told me it was because when they were in bed, he told her he didn't want to waste her time—that he loved her but didn't feel a real connection. He actually said, "One of us is going to get hurt, and it isn't going to be me."

Wow. Let me get this straight. This guy gets to have sex with you, calls you, comes over when he's horny, bored, or lonely—anytime he wants—and you just let him? You let him belittle you by basically telling you you're not good enough for him and that he's going to eventually dump you altogether when he finds a "real connection" with another woman? All this after you let him f@#k you?

OK, that's being pathetic. Even if he was worth being with, how can he have any respect for you if you just let him use you like that? And trust me, there's no shortage of men who will string a girl along so they can have sex and hang out whenever they feel like it—they just have to find a girl who'll let them.

⌒

"You know that little tingly feeling you get when you like someone? That's common sense leaving your body."

— (UNKNOWN)

⌒

I asked Stella how in the world she could say a guy like that was there for her. How could he be her rock? She was quiet for a minute and then chuckled a little and said, "For five years he's always been consistently partially there for me." Yes, that was her definition of a "rock." She actually thought it was love, and when she finally said it out loud, she realized how ridiculous it was. She was holding on to an exhaustingly shallow relationship because she was codependent and desperate for even the tiniest bit of affection from him. In her mind she believed she needed him.

She saw the light, and a few days later she texted me, "FYI, he still lives with his mom, and he only wears clothes with sports teams' logos on them. What have I been thinking?" She told him she was done.

A few weeks later, he called (they almost always do) and said, "OK, I can be with you, but I have to do my own thing on the weekends."

Stella said, "No, thanks," and hung up. She admitted to me a few months later that she let him come over for a few booty calls when she was feeling weak. Sometimes it takes a few more burns to finally take your hand out of the flame, even after you've seen him for what he's all about.

Some of you reading this might not be as obviously pathetic as Stella was, and some of you are possibly way more pathetic. Maybe he cuts you down here and there. Maybe he makes plans and flakes or says he's gonna call and doesn't. It doesn't matter how far gone you are. All that matters is that you're finally ready to take responsibility for your own happiness.

You know when you're being played, and you know when you're being pitiful. Just because he's a "nice guy" or "not ready" doesn't mean you need to waste any more time trying to convince him you'll be great together. You should never have to convince anyone to commit to you. The man in your life should be proud to have you as his partner. If he's not, he's not worth any more of your energy.

It's not always easy to let go of someone you've attached so much meaning to, but when you do the work to love yourself, you'll look back and have a good laugh at what you put up with and the stupid things you did to try to get a man to love you. When you have a sense of humor about how ridiculous you acted, you're finally ready to snap out of it.

⌒⌐

"It's not your job to like me. It's mine!"

— (BYRON KATIE)

⌒⌐

Brain Washed

CHAPTER 6

BRAINWASHED

BRAINWASHED BY A charmer?

Even if this isn't your situation, it happens for the same reason any dysfunctional relationship happens—lack of self-respect and insecurity. We've all seen it. The smart, beautiful girl is with a total jerk, and nobody understands why she's with him. She could have anyone she wants, but she's committed to some creepy guy who isn't even good to her.

I've seen girls from all backgrounds and childhoods in relationships like this. It's a mind-boggling phenomenon, and it always boils down to insecurity. Somehow the guy caught her attention and hooked her in with some endearing quality, usually humor or awkward charm. Once he has her hooked, he finds out what her insecurities are and subtly breaks her down. Before she knows it, she's a mess who is so emotionally broken she thinks she needs him to make her happy. Many times she has no idea he's even doing this. She thinks he's amazing and that she's lucky to have him!

～

"The most common way people give up their power is by thinking they don't have any

— (ALICE WALKER)

～

April was a total wreck when I met her—smart, hilarious, and one of the prettiest girls I've ever seen, but a complete hot mess. She was a corporate flight attendant, and pretty much every man who met her wanted her. She never even noticed, though. April was "in love" and in an incredibly dysfunctional, codependent relationship with a married man—a much older, very funny, charming, but manipulative married man. He was a Gulfstream pilot, and he'd helped get April her job.

April was only twenty-three and had just gone through a nasty divorce from her high school sweetheart when she met Don. She worked at a Starbucks in a small beach town outside of Los Angeles when she and Don became friends. She was new to the area, and Don seemed to know everyone. He wasn't good-looking at all, and he was way older than she was, but April loved the attention he gave her. He was so charismatic, and she felt special being around him during this lonely, confusing period of her life.

Their friendship deepened. He waited for April to go on break to sit and have coffee with her. He even brought his wife in to meet her! He said she was like a daughter to him and wanted them all to be friends. She went on trips with Don, his wife, and his young son. Yes, I know. So bizarre! His wife clearly had her own issues and was easily manipulated by Don as well.

Eventually, April and Don had an affair. The wife found out and decided to stay anyway. Apparently Don really knew how to pick suckers. He just stopped bringing April around the family home and social events, and instead stayed at her house a few nights a week.

April was so obsessed with Don that every morning she got up at 5:00 a.m., went for a run, showered, blow-dried her hair, and put on full makeup just in case Don decided to drop by that day. She wanted to look beautiful for him at all times. He subtly criticized her if she didn't look "perfect" and made little comments about her weight, so she was extra careful about how she looked and what she ate. She didn't care about his jabs, though. He was funny and fun and perfect in her eyes, so he must be right. She had her phone next to her 24-7 in case he called, and she always picked up on the first ring.

Don told April he couldn't leave his wife, who had been a virgin when she'd met her husband and so was a "saint" in his eyes. He insinuated that April was a slut because she wasn't a virgin, even though he was a fifty-five-year-old man having incredibly kinky sex with her. He wanted her to do things she was scared to do and that were way out of her comfort zone, but she was willing to do anything to make him happy.

She let herself become so manipulated that she even did his gardening at his family's vacation house. He dropped her off and picked her up down the street so nobody would see them. She told me these things, and I was mortified. The worst part is that she didn't even realize how bad it was. She was young and naïve, and she didn't have any close girlfriends to talk to. She was so dependent on this creep that she was completely brainwashed.

It took a few months of convincing, but she finally believed maybe this married, cheating knight in shining armor might not be good for her after all. She decided there was no way she could break it off cold turkey, so she started slowly. She thought she needed him and wasn't ready to let go completely, so the first baby step was to not pick up his call on the first ring. After a few weeks of that, she was ready to let his calls go to voicemail.

Don got irritated, and for the first time, April didn't care. She liked it. She confronted him about some of his lies. That started a little spark in her, and she saw through his manipulation. He wasn't staying with his wife because he felt bad or for the sake of his son—he stayed with her because he wanted to have both women. He enjoyed making them feel like they weren't good enough. He actually told April he didn't have sex with his wife anymore when he slept at home. Ha! Yeah, right. She finally saw him for the dirty old scumbag he was.

April went to her hometown to visit family and met a man. For the first time since she had known Don, she let herself open up enough to be interested in someone else. She was nervous, but she was ready to let go. This new man was kind and caring and completely different than Don. He and April fell in love.

April hadn't officially ended it with Don. She was avoiding him, but it was time to break the news. Don called her a whore and didn't believe she would go through with it. When he realized she was really leaving him for good, he had a complete meltdown. He couldn't eat or sleep. He told his wife he loved only April and got a divorce. He flew to April's parents' house to tell them he wanted to marry her. This happened all while April was planning a new life with her new man. The spell was broken.

Don finally got the hint and now tells anyone who will listen that April is a whore who ruined his marriage. Don's wife got remarried a year after their divorce, and April just had her first baby with her handsome, sweet new husband.

Now when I talk to April and bring up Don, she says it was like she was under a horrible spell. She was convinced she needed him and that she'd never be happy with anyone else. She feels like she woke up from a nightmare. Despite all that happened in that dysfunctional, bizarre relationship, April doesn't blame Don. She knows that if she'd respected herself and believed she was worth more, she would never have gotten into that situation.

"I used to think he took my breath away, but then I realized I was just being suffocated by his bullshit."

— (Unknown)

CHAPTER 7

CRAZY-MAKING PATTERNS

INSANITY IS DOING the same thing over and over while expecting a different result.

The way to break unhealthy patterns in relationships is to first notice them. Then figure out a plan to change, and stick to it. It's as simple as that. You don't need to pay a shrink five thousand dollars to tell you how shitty your childhood was or how your dad is a narcissist. If you want a man who treats you well and makes you a priority, but you keep falling for the party guy who can't even keep a job, it's time to change that pattern.

You're in a destructive pattern if every time you get in a relationship, you stop making plans with friends and make your boyfriend the center of your world until you finally smother him to death and he pulls away. Decide what kind of relationship you want and *be* the girl who deserves it.

Destructive patterns can even include how you present yourself to the world. The way you dress, how you act around men, and how you carry yourself are all reflections of how much you respect yourself. If you dress like a hooker and run around flirting with every man you meet, hoping to be swept away and taken care of, you're likely going to end up in a very shallow arrangement. You'll have to constantly play the part of a trophy to keep him interested. (Dressing sexy because you want to is different than dressing slutty because you need attention to feel good about yourself.)

Do you have patterns that could be holding you back from the kind of relationship you want? Do you give too much of yourself to men when you're dating? Do you go out of your way to get attention from men?

⸻

"If you treat me badly, it's OK! I'll do your laundry, laugh at your dumb jokes, and love you forever!"

— (LITTLE MISS PATHETIC)

⸻

Annie is a great example of a woman stuck in a toxic pattern of her own making. She's forty and has two kids. Her last real relationship was with a professional motocross guy named Ryan, and it lasted for ten years. The more she told me about him, the more I realized it was never actually a mutual relationship. Ryan told her not to tell anyone they were seeing each other, and he wouldn't go out in public with her as her boyfriend. They had to pretend they were friends.

Annie let this go on for as long as Ryan was willing to come over and have sex with her. She was so nuts over this guy that she told her kids to leave the house when he came over so she could sleep with him. When he left to hang out with his friends, her kids were allowed to come back home. Do you think this guy had any respect for Annie? Do you think Annie had any respect for herself? Needless to say, Ryan found a girl he does respect, and they're now married with a baby.

Ryan was no angel, and who knows what his marriage is like. But Annie set the stage for her unfulfilling, degrading time with Ryan. Annie still talks about him like he was the love of her life. She's still attracted to bad boys, but now they're younger than she is and disappear after just a few weeks. I try to explain all this to her, but she's stubborn and refuses to admit she's stuck in a pattern. Unless she notices and acknowledges her lack of self-respect and shallow attraction to the wrong men, she's never going to be happy with herself or anyone else.

Let's move on to the desperate husband catcher...

Janet is a great girl, but she might as well tie a noose around the neck of whomever she dates. She has a serious case of SYM (smother your man syndrome), and gets way too aggressive with the relationship claims before he's even fully committed. Men need to do the claiming! Men need the chance to court you and win you over. If you want to throw a fit and say that's sexist, keep on acting like a dude and see how far that gets you. Sorry, but it's just the way it is. Unless you want to be a dominating, aggressive woman who ends up with a wimpy, soft pushover, you need to let the man be a man.

Janet changed her relationship status on social media and put up memes about her "new man" that read, "I'm taken." She said, "I love you" before he did and told him how adorable and amazing he was. All this was doled out before the guy even had a chance to bond with her. Nobody wants to be with an overbearing, overexcited, forceful, overeager person, male or female. Desperation is the most unattractive quality in a potential partner. Be confident—let him pursue you.

If you've been dating the guy awhile and he doesn't move forward and you feel he's playing games or making excuses, tell him you think he's great but you're not interested in a half-assed relationship. Then move on. He'll either step up and commit, or he'll move on to the next girl. You'll save yourself a lot of grief and wasted time. Janet cannot seem to figure this out. She refuses to listen to any advice, continuing to do the same things over and over. She always gets dumped, and all her boyfriends say the same thing: "I'm not ready—you want more than I can give."

What they really mean is, "You're freaking me out and chasing me off with your desperation!"

"Don't be a woman who needs a man. Be a woman a man needs."

— (UNKNOWN)

Some girls just don't want to take responsibility for their circumstances. Many don't even think they act needy or desperate when they clearly do, and they keep being treated like crap or getting dumped over and over. Thankfully, if you've been reading this book, you're ready to change your ways. A woman in denial isn't able to get through the first chapter of this book—it doesn't even make sense to her.

The hardest part is admitting you've been acting ridiculous in your relationships. The rest is easy because now that you're aware of your mistakes, it's impossible to repeat them without catching yourself. You could fall back into some old habits, but you'll catch yourself and snap out of it pretty quickly. You'll consciously choose to no longer be a pathetic victim. I can't think of anything more rewarding than freeing yourself from the invisible chains of needing validation and approval from a man.

Let me make it clear that I love being a woman, but I'm not a feminist, and I'm not a proponent of the whole "war on women" that is often propagated by the media. Standing up for equal pay and gender equality where it is obviously necessary is needed, but to say there's a war on women in Western society today is quite a stretch and promotes the kind of victim mentality that could keep many women feeling like they can't rely on themselves to overcome an unfair or tough situation. That way of thinking is oppressive and counterproductive.

"This above all, refuse to be a victim."

— (MARGARET ATWOOD)

There unfortunately is an actual war on women in some dark parts of the world. Many women aren't allowed to make their own decisions. They can't show their faces to nonrelatives, drive a car, go out in public alone, or get a divorce, even from an abusive or cheating husband. They're considered second-class citizens with few rights and the "property" of men. Thankfully, in the West we can do, be, and have anything we want if we're willing to go for it.

The only thing holding women back in Western societies is themselves. So why do so many beautiful, talented women, with all the freedoms and all the opportunities in the world, willingly give themselves and their self-respect over to men? Why do so many women waste so much time trying to be accepted by men? I asked that question to several women who had been in dysfunctional relationships, and these are some of the answers I got:

- "I loved him and didn't want to lose him."
- "I was afraid of being alone."
- "I was afraid of not being loved."
- "I felt lost without a man."
- "It was embarrassing being the only single girl out of all my friends."
- "I was afraid I'd never get married and have kids."
- "I thought it was better to be with an asshole than to be single."
- "I thought I needed him to be happy."

The list goes on, but the answers are all basically the same. They're all based in fear, and none of them are good enough reasons to lose yourself and give away your dignity in a relationship. If you think trying to keep a man in a relationship based on your fear-driven insecurities will land you in a healthy, mutually loving situation, you're in for many rude awakenings.

Redirect that energy toward becoming a strong, secure woman who loves and honors herself. Choose to be with a man based on love and respect, not fear and desperation. You don't have to prove yourself to anyone. Trying to prove yourself to a man is degrading and exhausting. So stop that, and snap out of it! All you have to do is decide you're worth more.

"No one can make you feel inferior without your consent."

— (Eleanor Roosevelt)

Please walk all over me

CHAPTER 8

PLEASE WALK ALL OVER ME

NO MAN WILL ever respect a doormat.

A lot of women love the caretaker role. There's nothing wrong with that if you're with a great guy who loves, respects, and appreciates you and gives back in his own ways. But if you're with someone who isn't that into you and you're cooking for him, cleaning up after him, organizing his things, running errands for him, telling him how awesome he is, or putting him on a pedestal without getting much in return, someone needs to smack you upside the head. First of all, there's no reason to run around trying to make some guy happy when he doesn't do the same for you. Second, how is he ever going to respect you if you make him the center of your life and he doesn't have to lift a finger?

If you don't like being a doormat, then get off the floor

— (AL ANON)

People appreciate what they earn. If he hasn't earned your love by treating you well and showing you how much you mean to him, put his dirty socks back where he left them. Take a step back and ask yourself why you feel the need to be his assistant, maid, and cheerleader. Are you trying to show him what a great wife you'd be and how hard you'll work to make him happy? How's that working out for you? Not so great, right?

Men don't fall in love with ass-kissing housekeepers. They don't want a slave or a mommy or an errand girl. Some will certainly take advantage of it if you offer it up, but they'll never treat you well. They'll let you wash their underwear and buy groceries as long as you're willing to do it, but don't bring up commitment or respect—because being a guy's doormat and gaining his respect will never go together.

Is there an "open for service" sign on your bedroom door?

Sex is great. We all love it, and we all do it. If you don't, you're either saving yourself (good for you!) or you're not into it. If it's the latter, you might want to get a bunch of cats and forget about relationships. Life will be a lot less complicated for you!

Sex with someone you love, and who loves you back, is amazing. It doesn't get any better. When a man is committed and you love and respect each other, sex is a beautiful thing. Having sex with someone who isn't emotionally present in the relationship is a different story. You might think it's awesome, and maybe it's fun, but it's empty fun. You're trying to be sexy and turn him on so he keeps coming back. After it's over, what is there? More sex.

The only thing holding you both together is physical manipulation. There's no feeling of safety and being loved. There's no talk of the future, just the next performance. You'll want more from him and eventually break up. Then he'll miss having his convenient noncommittal arrangement, so he'll reel you back in, and you'll hope things will be different. The makeup sex will be fun and exciting, but after a few weeks or months, you'll feel just as empty as the last time.

Stop trying to keep him by having sex with him. Respect yourself, and take care of yourself. Only become intimate with him if he proves he's seriously in love with you. You'll know when someone really respects and loves you. If you're not a priority to him, spend your time elsewhere.

⌒

"Your body is a temple, not a visitor center."

— (UNKNOWN)

⌒

For some reason many women think if they give a man good sex whenever he wants, he'll love them forever. Sometimes sex is the only time they actually feel close to the guy they're dating because it's the only time there seems to be intimacy. Since they aren't in a healthy relationship, they don't communicate in any way that is meaningful. Sex becomes a manipulation to keep him hooked, and they trick themselves into thinking he'll change one day because he must love and care for them if he keeps wanting sex.

News flash! We live on a planet packed with men who would be more than willing to sleep with you if you make yourself available, no matter how they feel about you. I have spoken to several men who say they do not view sex as an emotional act the way women often do. It seems women are more likely to become emotionally attached during and after sex, while men are more likely to view sex as a physical urge.

It's just easier for these men to separate sex and love. It's not necessarily a bad thing. It's just how many men are wired. Knowing that should make it easier for women to avoid using sex as a way to try and make men love them. A good man will respect you for waiting until he's committed—even if you've already slept with the man you're seeing. If he won't commit, do yourself a favor and stop. You've heard the saying, "Why buy the cow when you can get the milk for free?" I'm guessing a woman didn't make that up.

Jess becomes a cute and attentive little doormat...

Jess is a sweetheart! Everyone who meets her absolutely loves her. She's a pretty little blonde with a great personality, and she's always there for anybody who needs her. Jess has no problem finding men. Men love her because she's adorable and easygoing, but too soon into the relationship, she dives in headfirst and succumbs to the relationship destroying affects of smother your man syndrome. She starts buying her man things, pays for dinners, goes out of her way to make everything really convenient, and is just overly available. Her man is priority over all else. She senses she's being too available, so she tries to play cool or act busy, but her desperation to please is transparent even when she pretends to have plans or backs off. Even if she makes real plans, she constantly thinks about the guy. Jess can make herself seem as busy and removed as she wants, but she's not fooling anyone. SYM syndrome is about the energy you are putting out. Nothing can hide desperation, not even faking happiness. Your desperation will show through no matter how you communicate.

Jess always sleeps with men before any sort of commitment is established. She becomes a glorified booty call very quickly, and the guys think she's awesome. They love hanging out with her, and they think she's really nice, but they always tell her they aren't ready for a relationship and string her along for months, sometimes years. One guy owes her twenty thousand dollars! She let him buy a truck in her name, and now she has to call him every month and track him down to make the payment. She almost got a boob job just to make this guy happy.

The guy Jess was seeing for the past year recently broke it off with her. He never called her his girlfriend, and he kept himself too busy to commit. She always talked about how great he was. She told me he was amazing and really sweet. She said he was so open and honest, that he was a really good communicator. He was just too busy, she reasoned. She claimed he wasn't ready yet because he wasn't in a good place. *No, Jess!* If a man wants to be with a woman, nothing will stop him from being with her.

The reason he was too busy and wasn't ready was because Jess went out of her way to please him even when he didn't return her texts. He didn't consider her his girlfriend or make her a priority in any way besides sex and the need to boost his ego. She drove to his house and slept with him whenever he wanted, even if she had plans or was tired from working all day. Jess was pretty much always available for him for anything, anytime. She cleaned his house, did his yard work, and fed his cat.

One time this guy didn't return her texts all day, and what did Jess do? She bought him lunch and took it to his work. When she got to his office, they said he had just left. Jess ended up giving his lunch to the receptionist. I almost had a heart attack when she told me this! That was normal for her. She thought that if she did nice things for him and treated him like a king, he would want her. It doesn't work that way.

Women are natural caretakers. We like doing nice things for people we love, but when you're giving yourself and your time to a man who isn't that into you, you just end up feeling used and unappreciated because men don't *really* want a caretaker. They want a strong, confident woman who respects herself.

The problem is Jess didn't respect herself. Her guy knew he didn't treat her right. She didn't care, though. She was willing to settle for crumbs, and that's basically man repellent. If you stick around and try to please a guy who half-asses a relationship, he'll never respect you. He'll tell you you're amazing and great, but that he just isn't ready. You'll find out later he has a girlfriend and is in love. Yup. That's the way it goes.

As I mentioned earlier, this guy did break it off with Jess. They were never official, but it gets comfortable for men to have a girl always available, especially a sweet, loving girl who's fun to hang out with and will have sex whenever.

Jess is getting better. She sees the pattern, and she's ready to respect herself in a relationship. She's ready to be with someone who treats her as well as she treats him. She promised herself she'll never again be a housekeeper, gardener, or moneylender for a man she's dating. She is realizing that happiness doesn't come from outside herself. Finding self-worth and security is an inside job.

⌒

"When a woman becomes her own best friend life is easier."

— (DIANE VON FURSTENBERG)

⌒

CHAPTER 9

SORRY, NOT SORRY

THE ONE THING that's inevitable in all relationships, but especially in unhealthy, codependent, or one-sided relationships, is that the person feeling unappreciated or used is going to get really emotional and have a meltdown at some point, maybe even often. The worst thing you can do after an emotional or angry conversation, whether via text, voicemail, e-mail, or in person, is to apologize for getting upset. If your feelings were hurt and you overreacted, the only thing you need to say is that you were upset and could have communicated better—but *never* apologize for the way you feel. That just means you don't own your feelings and aren't confident enough to stand up for yourself.

Here's a good example of my friend Cindy saying sorry and totally disrespecting herself to get Tony to talk to her again.

As with most of these relationships, Tony was infatuated with Cindy at the start. He acted like her boyfriend right away. Then about a month in, he got "really busy." He flaked on Cindy, took hours to text her back, showed up when it was convenient, and usually didn't refer to her as his girlfriend. Cindy made little remarks about how he was too busy for her and asked why he was treating her differently. That just annoyed Tony, and he got even more distant. He liked her but felt like her world revolved around him, and it freaked him out. But like most men, he never just came out and said that.

Instead, he simply avoided Cindy unless he was horny or bored.

One night, Tony was supposed to come over, but as usual, he texted that he was tired and probably wouldn't see her that week because he was busy. Cindy had had enough. She was *pissed*, and she went to her "crazy place." She texted him back: "F#!k off. I'm over this crap. I'm sick of you coming and going whenever you please like I have a revolving door in my bedroom. You won't even commit to me, so I have no time for this BS anymore." She included a lot more names and swear words too.

Tony didn't know what to say. He thought it was kind of funny, and he didn't write back. Cindy was fine with that. She was over him…for about two hours. Then she felt bad. She thought about how sweet Tony used to be and reasoned that he really was just tired. He worked so hard, and she was so mean…*blah, blah, blah.* And that's how the pathetic apologies happen.

⌒

**"There are only two types of women—goddesses
and doormats."**

— (PABLO PICASSO)

⌒

Cindy had written in that text exactly how she felt, so why did she feel a need to apologize? She was tired of feeling used. She was always waiting around for Tony and making excuses for the way he treated her. Little did she know that was part of what made Tony so distant. He knew she'd always be there, no matter what he did or how he acted. So when Cindy texted Tony less than a day after her angry text tirade and apologized, telling him she shouldn't have gotten upset and that she missed him, he lost even more respect for her. He went right back to acting the way he had before, coming over when he wanted some action and ignoring her when he felt she was too annoying.

Everything Cindy had texted was true to her feelings. Sure, she freaked out and went a little overboard. She definitely could have gotten her point across in a much more productive way and she's working on that now, but she was being authentic in that moment the best way she knew how. If she had owned it and respected herself, she would have been well on her way to snapping out of it. But she belittled herself and her integrity by apologizing for being upset. She owed Tony no excuses about what she was feeling, and she was *finally* acting like she had some backbone. Strong women don't apologize for how they feel, and if a man doesn't respect that, he's not valuing your worth.

Once you begin standing up for yourself, you'll quickly realize how much better it feels. When you decide to put yourself first, you get more confidence in your relationships. You stop making the guy you're dating the center of your universe and take care of yourself. Being needy makes you seem desperate, and men can sense desperation. You might as well have a flashing sign on your head that reads, "Hi! You can treat me like shit!"

Tony eventually fell for a girl who didn't have a job and wasn't nearly as cute or as smart as Cindy, but guess what—she respected herself and didn't put up with any crap. She was a strong girl with a bit of an attitude, and it took that breakup for Cindy to figure out that being a doormat is not only extremely unattractive to men, but it's also a miserable way to live your life.

"People who want the most approval get the least and people who need approval the least get the most."

— (WAYNE DYER)

CHAPTER 10

BOUNDARIES

WE ALL HAVE the ability to choose how to react to our circumstances. We were all born with that gift. And it really is a gift! No matter what situation we're in, we decide how to respond. We can set personal boundaries to protect ourselves and our integrity, and we can live our lives by our own internal compasses.

When you don't have your own clear boundaries to retain your self-respect and integrity, you rely on others to decide your boundaries for you. This goes for all aspects of your life, from work to friendships to parenting. In relationships this is especially dangerous because you expect your partner to know how to treat you. Just because you might think something he says or does is rude or hurtful doesn't mean he thinks it is. And even if he meant to be rude, it's usually how you react that determines how far things escalate.

Instead of calmly telling him how you feel and why, you might become passive-aggressive, hold it in, or throw a tantrum. All these reactions make it obvious that you expect him to know your boundaries and that you're not willing to set your own. If you are levelheaded and respect your own boundaries, it's easy to communicate how you feel. This helps you both learn how to be a good partner to each other. If he continues to say or do things that are hurtful after you've let him know how you feel, you're with a guy who doesn't value you, and girls who respect themselves don't waste time on men who won't respect their boundaries.

⌒⟶

"A lack of boundaries invites a lack of respect."

— (UNKNOWN)

⌒⟶

How do you know when someone crosses your boundaries, and how do you know when you're overreacting? I love to give examples because it's so easy to relate to real stories. I know two women who were in similar situations but reacted completely differently and had completely different outcomes—all because of their differences in determining and expressing boundaries.

First, meet Lilly and Brian…

Lilly has come so far. She's only twenty-one, but levelheaded and always wanting to better herself. Her problem used to be that she worried about everything her on-and-off-again boyfriend, Brian, said or did, but she never told him how she felt. He got away with a lot because she never expressed her feelings. He ignored her and did not return texts.

He would tell her that she was so easy to be around and he liked that she never got emotional. This made it even harder for Lilly to communicate her feelings to Brian because she wanted him to think she was "cool" and thought that telling him how she felt would annoy him.

After many long e-mail and Skype conversations (she lives in New Zealand), she learned how to communicate with Brian. I explained to her that asking for what she wants did not mean she would be whining or getting emotional. If something he did or said caused her to feel uncomfortable, she should let him know in a direct, mature way. She didn't have to complain or cry to get her point across. She just needed to decide what she wanted and explain to him calmly and confidently. Most men don't respond well to emotionally charged communication. They're usually rational and to the point. If you come at them upset about something without knowing what you want, they'll likely shut down and avoid or get angry. You might not always get the outcome you want, but if you take the emotion out and make the decision to respect your integrity and communicate rationally, no matter what the outcome, you'll feel good about it. Lilly decided she would never again sacrifice her integrity so someone else would accept her. Now they're committed, and every time I hear from her, she seems more and more confident. She now knows she'll be happy with or without Brian, and he has definitely reacted positively to Lilly's newfound self-respect. He's become a really good boyfriend.

Not long after Lilly began asserting herself, they had an inevitable bump in the relationship road. Lilly found a text from another girl on Brian's phone. It was a girl who had flirted with him before, someone he'd known before Lilly was his girlfriend. Brian wrote her back something a little too friendly, and it freaked Lilly out. Lilly didn't confront him right away because she knew she'd get really emotional if she confronted him before she calmed down. Everything had been going so well, and now she was devastated. It took her a few hours to gain perspective. She called me to ask if she was overreacting.

This was a really good time to identify and respect her boundaries. I asked her if she wanted to be with a man who texted other women behind her back. If not, would she be willing to lose Brian to keep her integrity and respect her boundaries? Because in the end, the most important thing is that she respects herself, even if that means letting go of someone she loves. If you don't stick to your boundaries, you'll never have a successful relationship anyway, so you might as well live with integrity and know your worth. She decided she was willing to lose Brian if he could disrespect her like that.

That's how you want to go into a serious conversation—with no fear. You can love someone but still be willing to lose him if he doesn't treat you right. When she confronted Brian, she calmly but firmly told him she'd seen the text and that if corresponding with other women who flirt with him was something he felt the need to do, she wasn't interested in being in a relationship with him. She said, "I love you, Brian, but that's not going to work for me. I have no interest in being with a man who wants that kind of attention from other women while in a relationship."

Brian's jaw dropped. He had never seen Lilly react so rationally while standing up for herself, and he was blown away. He felt so stupid. He apologized over and over, and for the first time, he realized he could lose her. They're both young, and that's why I think it is especially important for Lilly to learn to communicate with Brian. She's setting the stage for her future with Brian or any other man she decides to be with.

I wish I'd known how to recognize and identify my boundaries and communicate when I was Lilly's age. I would have saved myself decades of frustration.

⌁

"I would rather be alone with dignity than in a relationship that requires me to sacrifice my self-respect."

— (MANDY HALE)

⌁

Now meet Kassandra and John...

Kassandra didn't know how to identify her boundaries and calmly communicate them to John. It was Kassandra's birthday, and she was sure John would do something special for her. She told all her friends she couldn't make plans because John was probably going to surprise her. Well, John came over but didn't surprise her and barely mentioned her birthday. She was sad and hurt but didn't say anything.

Kassandra's very pretty neighbor happened to come over, crying because her beloved dog had run away. Kassandra had a sprained ankle and couldn't be much help, so she asked John to help the neighbor look for the dog. John has always been a really helpful guy, and he stayed out posting signs until well after dinnertime. Kassandra was fuming. Not only did John do nothing for her birthday, but he also spent four hours helping another woman. It didn't matter that Kassandra told him to go. She felt he should have come back ASAP and done something special for her or at least taken her to dinner.

When John walked in the door, Kassandra was about to explode. She screamed at John, acted jealous, told him to go f#^k the neighbor, and so on. Kassandra's tantrums about her birthday went on for weeks, and John was ready to give up. He felt there was nothing he could do to make her happy, and when a man feels that way, it's pretty much over. John knew he'd made a mistake, but listening to Kassandra call him names and lose her mind over and over without even trying to communicate was too much for him. They broke up a few months later.

The first personal boundary Kassandra ignored and John crossed was when John didn't do anything nice for her birthday. She didn't say anything, even though she was really hurt. That set the stage for the rest of the night. The second boundary crossed was John staying out for four hours with the neighbor when he should have spent maybe half an hour helping and then gone back to Kassandra's to celebrate her birthday.

Instead of confronting him about his lack of planning, she tried to be cool and keep quiet. Even though she felt awful and wanted to cry, she acted like everything was fine and told him to go help the neighbor. All she really wanted was to go to dinner with her boyfriend for her birthday. John was an idiot, and often men do really dumb things that contribute to a woman's temporary insanity. But this whole scenario would have played out much differently if Kassandra had honored her feelings and communicated them to John. She could have told him she was looking forward to spending her birthday with him. Instead, John thought she wasn't really into birthdays. His family didn't make a big deal about them, so he assumed it was the same for Kassandra. He thought he was being a nice guy by helping the neighbor like she asked. Instead of calmly working all this out, Kassandra took the victim route and became an emotional wreck, eventually driving John away. She continued calling and texting, trying to get John back, but he decided she was emotionally fragile and too much work for him.

Oh, John and the neighbor did find the dog. At least something good came of that day.

Hopefully Kassandra will snap out of it one day. She's coming around, but still blames John for their breakup.

You know someone has overstepped one of your boundaries when you physically feel hurt by something someone else has done or said. Some people say they feel punched in the stomach when they find out their man lied about something. Or you might feel sick when you're called a name or talked to a certain way. It's as simple as that. Many women's reactions are to get emotional and dramatic, yell and cry, or call all their friends and complain about how someone has wronged them.

It's the easy way out to act like a victim and feel sorry for yourself, but there are more productive ways to deal with your emotions. When someone has crossed the line and you truly want to resolve things, before you start any discussion, you'll get a lot more out of the conversation after you calm yourself down. A woman confronting a man when she's mad or crying is about as useful as speaking pig Latin to a two-year-old. Men will stare at you blankly, shut down, or get defensive, and you'll be even more upset.

Decide what you want and what it will take to continue a relationship with a man while respecting yourself and your values. Figure out what your boundaries are and why you feel that way. Have a calm and direct conversation, knowing you'll be fine. As long as you respect your limits and values, you're always doing the right thing—even if that means ending a relationship. You are *always* better off staying true to yourself.

If you have a good man, he'll love you even more for setting boundaries because it shows how much you love yourself. Confidence is irresistible. If he doesn't respect how you feel, it's up to you to move on. Don't stick around feeling sorry for yourself, expecting things to change. If you don't respect yourself, he certainly never will.

⌒

"A beautiful woman is a confident woman."

— (PATRICIA BONALDI)

⌒

CHAPTER 11

BOOMERANG

THE IDEA OF forgiving is really hard for some people, especially in relationships. If you've been lied to, cheated on, or treated badly, it can be challenging to just say, "No biggie—all is forgiven." I've never been one to hold on to grudges or stay angry at someone, but I did have a hard time letting go of someone I cared about, no matter how badly he treated me. Even if I hadn't talked to him in months, I thought about him and got sad about things that had happened or wondered what he was doing, if he ever thought about me, and if he was dating anyone.

I think most women obsess a little over an ex because we're just way more emotionally driven than men. Plus, now we have so many different ways to see what someone is up to that it's almost impossible not to do a little sneaky cyberstalking. Holding a grudge and holding on to the past are basically the same, whether you're angry or nostalgic. It's so hard for some women to let go of a person they cared so much for. Even if you're in a relationship that's on and off, when it's off it can feel like a death.

I don't like to use the word *forgive* because I don't think the forgiveness process really works for most people when it comes to exes, not to mention it's next to impossible if you're dealing with a difficult breakup. Letting go is a lot of work, and sometimes that word just sounds too generic and one-dimensional for a complex breakup or long-term relationship issue.

The best way to move on and let go of someone takes a little courage, but it's really simple. In fact, it's so simple that sometimes your mind will go crazy trying to make it complicated, but here it is:

When you think about him, wish him well.

Yes, wish him well! You can call it sending blessings, good vibes, or good energy, but the most important thing is that even though you might feel hurt or sad, you'll heal and even thrive when you truly wish him well. This might sound weird and New Agey, but trust me, miracles happen when you do this. It literally comes back to you like a boomerang, and you set yourself and him free.

It's true that what you wish for someone else you give to yourself. This is different than forgiving because you don't have to sit and think about all the shitty things he did and try to figure out how to come to terms with the situation. He's only human, and those things are in the past. This way you can throw the baby out *with* the bathwater and wipe your hands of it. No need to forgive because you skip all that and choose to move on completely, with nothing but good thoughts. The past is over and done with.

This doesn't mean you condone bad behavior or that you're a pushover. You're just choosing a better path. If you constantly think bad thoughts about him or obsess over what he's doing, all that negativity, like a boomerang, comes straight back to you. You feel bad because you think about the bad things he's done, or you feel lonely because you obsess over him and what he's doing or who he's doing it with.

Just disconnect from the negative things that have happened. Accept and take responsibility for your own happiness from now on, and in your heart wish him well. Then let go and know you're going to be fine. You get strength from rising above destructive thoughts and letting go of old negative patterns. Nothing good ever comes of petty or obsessive negative thinking, even if you feel it's justified. You reap what you sow. Once again, like a boomerang, it always comes back to you.

Don't, I repeat, *do not* text, e-mail, or call him to tell him you're thinking good thoughts about him or that you're sending him blessings. You'll sound like a nut, and it could get weird. This is something you do just for yourself, by yourself.

Decide to be a positive force. Wish him well when you think of him. Just picture him happy, and know that you'll also be happy. You both shared a special part of your lives with each other. You'll always be connected because of that, but set him free and send him love so you'll be free and able to receive love. If the relationship is really meant to be, you'll be together again when the time is right.

Please remember you are an amazing, unique, beautiful person, and you should never let someone—or even your thoughts about someone—bring you down and distract you from who you are and what you have to offer the world. If you don't believe that about yourself, figuring it out is a great way to start your new journey—free from letting your happiness and worth depend on something outside of yourself.

⌒

**"Happiness depends on being free, and freedom
depends on being courageous."**

— (THUCYDIDES)

⌒

Take your life back !

CHAPTER 12

SNAPPING OUT OF IT!

IF YOU'VE BEEN stuck in a pattern of feeling sorry for yourself, blaming someone else, and acting like a victim, it can take some convincing to believe you're actually in control of your own confidence. You handed it over to someone who should never have had that kind of control in the first place. Nobody should be in control of someone else's self-worth. Couples aren't supposed to latch on and rely on each other for their happiness. When you see a happy relationship, it's always two people who love and respect each other but are totally happy with themselves. Many marriages end because one (or both) expects too much from the other.

If you aren't happy with yourself, you redirect your discontent onto the person you are closest to and blame him for your misery. Everything he does is frustrating to you. How exhausting is that? Focusing on and blaming others is just a sneaky, manipulative way of ignoring your own issues. If you love yourself and have healthy self-confidence, you don't waste time obsessing over what others are doing. Look away from them and look at yourself.

Instead of thinking you can change someone or need someone to make you happy, put all that energy into figuring out what makes you *you*. Enjoy yourself and who you are. If a man drives you crazy, take the wheel and drive someplace a lot more fulfilling.

You might put a lot of your goals and to-dos on the back burner while you obsess over every word your man has said, done, texted, Instagrammed, Snapchatted, Facebooked, tweeted, or e-mailed. Most of us end up playing dead-end scenarios out in our heads, and that takes a lot of time from our days and our lives, but nothing ever comes of it. You end up stuck in a zero-growth pattern. Nothing seems fun, work is neglected, chores pile up, and friends have fun without you because you're a Debbie Downer. Life starts to feel empty because you're just pretending to have fun or stay busy while you wait for his next text or obsess over what you wish he would say or do for you.

The best way I've found to reprogram my drama-addicted brain into a healthy, confident brain is to take care of myself. You've probably neglected yourself for so long that you don't even know what makes you happy anymore. Or maybe you know what makes you happy, but you don't have the inspiration or desire to do it.

One easy thing to do is go online to look up inspiring sayings and quotes. This might sound silly, but trust me, when you read quotes that inspire you and you focus on them every day instead of repeating your old destructive patterns, your brain wakes up and reprograms itself. Therapists call this a form of cognitive behavioral therapy. It can help you outthink negative patterns you've been repeating.

Collect quotes that make you feel strong and happy. Just Google quotes about loving yourself, self-confidence, self-respect, and so forth. Take screenshots of the ones that really resonate with you. Only save those that make you feel strong and hopeful. Put them in a folder or locked photo album app you can download onto your phone. I've added lots of inspiring quotes in this book for you to highlight or photograph. In a different album, save photos of places you want to visit, goals you have, and people doing things you want to do one day. If you're ready to get into another relationship, write down all the qualities you want in a man. It's really helpful to have a clear picture of the ideal type of relationship you want to be in in the future. Stay inspired, change your quotes and photos, and add to them as often as you need. Look forward to your exciting life ahead.

"Imagination is everything. It is the preview of life's coming attractions."

— (ALBERT EINSTEIN)

Before you go to bed, when you wake up, and anytime you feel yourself getting sucked back into a negative vibe, take a few minutes to read your quotes and look at your photos. Close your eyes and imagine yourself as confident and happy, doing the things you love. It doesn't matter if you're overweight, miserable, broke, or depressed. You can use your imagination to take you where you want to be. The more you do this, the more your brain will get used to happy thoughts as you open up to new experiences and opportunities.

Being miserable is much harder than being happy. You just forgot how easy it is to be happy! To be happy, all you need are self-confidence and an imagination—things you were born with. So stop your brain from being miserable, and have fun with your thoughts.

"Change your thoughts and you change your world."

— (NORMAN VINCENT PEALE)

Another way to put the focus back onto yourself is to replace an old destructive or time-wasting habit with a positive, healthy habit.

Jennifer used to wake up first thing in the morning and go straight to her phone. She watched her texts for any sign of Mr. Wonderful and checked all his social media posts and his friends' posts to make sure he wasn't up to anything. She went through all her e-mails and all her friends' social media. It took forty-five minutes to an hour just to get out of bed because she wasted so much time on this ritual.

This was a big problem, and she was dying to break the bad habit. Jennifer decided to take up running. Now she lays her exercise clothes and tennis shoes out the night before, and the first thing she does in the morning is get dressed, stretch, and go for a run. She was in really bad shape, so she started out slow. She said little old ladies walked as fast as she jogged, but she stuck with it. She ran half a mile and walked half a mile the first three weeks. The most important thing was to get out of bed with a positive goal instead of starting her day with the stress of worrying about someone else.

Within the first week, Jennifer was thinking more clearly. She was getting oxygen to her brain and working her muscles instead of stressing herself out and having anxiety first thing in the morning. When she ran, she decided she would be in the moment and focus on her body and how it felt to move and breathe instead of weight loss as her main goal.

Three months later she's running three miles, five days a week, and doing yoga a few nights a week. She also eats more healthfully, and her whole outlook has changed. She takes care of herself instead of cyberstalking her man every day.

Take a break from the chatter in your head.

"I think I think too much."

— (IDINA MENZEL)

This goes for most people, but if you're in an unhealthy relationship, your poor brain is working overtime. Its obvious stress comes from your thoughts. If you don't think the stressful thoughts, you can't be stressed. Stress greatly increases the probability of depression, Alzheimer's disease, heart disease, diabetes, asthma, and just about every other disease in the human body.

Obviously, it's impossible to go around all day without thinking, but there's a way to calm your crazy thoughts. Yes, I'm going to say it—meditation.

I used to think meditation was for people who look like they need a shower and wear socks with sandals. I thought you needed beads and bells and excessive hair to get into meditation, but actually the basic concept is simple and valuable for everyone if you take all the New Ageness out of it. Meditation is really just learning how to quiet your mind. People use drugs, alcohol, and prescription medication to avoid their thoughts and stressful lives, but meditation is something *anyone* can do for free, and it's scientifically proven to reduce stress.

I did a little research and found some of the most talented, most successful people in the world meditate. In fact, twenty million people in the United States meditate every day, including Oprah, Ellen, Rupert Murdoch, Russell Simmons, Clint Eastwood, Jerry Seinfeld, professional athletes, politicians, and the list goes on. They've all stated that meditation gives them more focus and keeps them calm in stressful situations. These are people who can afford to incorporate any means of stress reduction into their lives, but what do they do? A free technique that we all have the ability to utilize and anyone can do almost anywhere.

**"The soul always knows what to do to heal itself.
The challenge is to silence the mind."**

— (CAROLINE MYSS)

There are a ton of videos, books, and articles on how to meditate. Different techniques work for different people. Try a few to see which works best for your busy brain. It's a mind exercise. Think of your mind as a muscle—with time, your brain gets stronger and better at meditating, so be sure to stick with it. Our bodies need nutritious food and exercise to stay healthy, and we brush and floss our teeth to keep our gums healthy. Doesn't it make sense to take care of the brain's health?

It's impossible to love life and have passion if you're constantly worried about someone else. Relationships aren't always easy, but they should be supportive and, most of all, mutually respectful. Self-worth is an inside job. Don't wake up five or ten years from now and realize you were just chasing misery!

"Some women chase men, others chase dreams."

— (LADY GAGA)

Smoking, drinking excessively, watching too much TV, and scrolling through social media all day are all just wastes of time and ways to avoid focusing on oneself. Think of something challenging and rewarding you can do to replace your bad habits. If you change your patterns, your life changes for the better very quickly. It can be challenging to let go of bad habits. They're like little warm security blankets, but they always do more harm than good and distract you from who you really are.

You just need to decide to change and believe in yourself. Meditate, exercise, read inspiring quotes, and focus on your goals to visualize a better, healthier version of yourself. Before you know it, you'll gravitate toward people and situations that bring you happiness. It took you a while to get into this funk, so give yourself time to bounce back from it. Have fun with this. Obsessing over a relationship seems like a big waste of time when you love your life.

"One of the happiest moments in life is when you find the courage to let go of what you can't change."

— (JOHN GREEN)

CHAPTER 12 ½

ONE LAST THING

I GOT A phone call the other day from a girl who's in a relationship that has improved drastically because she snapped out of it. Like I said earlier, this doesn't always happen, but it's pretty common. He has done a complete turnaround and loves how confident she's become. They're a cute, happy couple now, but she called to ask if I thought it would last. Will he go back to not making her a priority and treating her poorly? Here's what I told her, and this advice applies to everyone: Of course he will. It's very likely he'll have a bad day or even a bad week. What matters most is how you react and how you feel about yourself. I know of very few relationships that don't have ups and downs. Assuming you're not with a sociopath or abusive egomaniac, it's your reaction to frustrating behavior that determines the outcome—and your level of self-respect determines your reactions.

So basically I told her it doesn't matter as long as she maintains her integrity. A guy can disappear, and if you truly are strong and confident, you'll get over him. That's what really matters. You know exactly how to communicate your feelings now, and if he doesn't like it, tell him you've got better things to do and go get a manicure. If he's a good guy who's having a bad day, he'll apologize and fix his behavior. If he continues to be disrespectful and rude, ask yourself if it's worth it to stay with someone who doesn't care enough to treat you well. Just in case you forgot everything in this book, the answer is no...hell, no! We only get to live this life once, and it goes by in a flash. Stand up for yourself and don't waste anymore of your time on people whose love and loyalty you have to constantly question.

"If you don't like the road you're walking, start paving another one."

— (DOLLY PARTON)

Remember to love yourself

Thank you for reading *Girl, Snap Out Of It!*

We invite you to share your thoughts and reactions

Please go to our amazon page : **Girl, Snap Out Of It!**
to leave your review

https://www.amazon.com/Girl-Snap-Out-Relationship-Madness-ebook/dp/B01FTHLJIA?ie=UTF8&keywords=girl%20snap%20out%20of%20it&qid=1464202818&ref_=sr_1_1&s=books&sr=1-1#customerReviews

girlsnapoutofit.com – Facebook – Instagram – Twitter

CPSIA information can be obtained
at www.ICGtesting.com
Printed in the USA
LVOW11s0937201116

513797LV00002B/369/P